prima
CRAFTS

BAKING

OVER 25 BAKING AND CAKE DECORATING IDEAS FOR EVERY OCCASION

prima CRAFTS BAKING

D&C

David and Charles

www.stitchcraftcreate.co.uk/ideas

Contents

Introduction

With over 600,000 readers *Prima* is a successful women's general interest magazine. Crafts are one of the most important aspects of the magazine and the free monthly pattern is as popular today as it was 27 years ago when *Prima* was first launched. The craft pages aim to please all levels of expertise and cover a wide range of crafts, including knitting, sewing, patchwork and embroidery, as well as many other creative ideas for you and your home. *Prima's* craft experts appeal to different generations and the magazine has successfully adapted to suit the current resurgence in crafting. From five minutes to five hours, *Prima's* projects satisfy makers of all ages.

The Editor

Prima Magazine

London

Beautiful Birdie Biscuits
by Ruth Clemens

YOU WILL NEED:

♥ Circular biscuits
  (7.5cm/3in diameter)

♥ White, blue, purple
  and pink sugarpaste

♥ Pink, purple, golden yellow
  and black royal icing

♥ Fluted cookie cutter and
  small round cutter

♥ Petal cutters
  Large, small and extra
  small rose petal

1. Roll out the white sugarpaste to 3mm (⅛in) thick; cut out a fluted circle. Secure to the top of a biscuit using a little water.

2. Roll out the blue sugarpaste to 2mm (³⁄₃₂in) thick; cut out the bird's body using the large petal cutter and use the small round cutter to cut out the bird's head. Roll out the purple sugarpaste to 2mm (³⁄₃₂in) thick and cut out three tail feathers with the extra small petal cutter. Set aside.

3. Roll out the pink sugarpaste, to 2mm (³⁄₃₂in) thick and cut out a small petal for the bird's wing. Pinch the thin end of the petal and curve the shape slightly to create the curve of the wing. Use a knife to mark three lines along the wing.

4. Start to build the bird onto the biscuit using the pieces you have cut out. Start with the tail feathers securing them in position with a dab of water. Add the body, the head and finally the wing.

5. Using the black royal icing, pipe a dot for the bird's eye and two legs. Add a beak with golden yellow royal icing.

6. Finally pipe three pink bulbs between the bird's feet and tail feathers and three purple bulbs to the right of the bird's head.

Little Pot Cupcakes

by Zoe Scott

YOU WILL NEED:

- ♥ Cake mixture
- ♥ Six-cup king size muffin tin
- ♥ Lily and leaf cutter set
- ♥ Silver edible lustre spray
- ♥ Buttercream
- ♥ White, yellow and green sugarpaste
- ♥ Grey food colouring

1. Grease, then line the muffin tin with 12 strips of greaseproof paper 20cm (7⅞in) long arranged in crosses in each hole of the tin. Pour in the cake mixture and bake until it springs back to the touch. Allow to cool slightly, then use the paper to remove. Once the muffins have cooled, set one aside; spread buttercream over the other five, covering all the sides, using a palette knife to smooth the surface.

2. Take 500g (2lb 2oz) of sugarpaste, colour grey and roll out on a surface dusted with icing sugar. Cut strips approximately 30cm x 10cm (11⅞in x 3⅞in) wide and wrap around the muffin smoothing as you go. Use the base of the muffin tin to cut circles of grey for the pot base and 2cm (¾in) wide strips to wrap around for the rim of the pot. Spray the 'pots' all over with the silver lustre spray. Allow to dry.

3. Using the set aside muffin, crumble and sprinkle over the top of the pots for 'soil'.

4. Using the lily cutter and former, cut petals from rolled out yellow sugarpaste and gently press into place to make the flowers. Use the leaf cutters to make leaves from green sugarpaste. Place the flowers and leaves on the 'soil'.

Superstar Cake Pops
by James Brooks

YOU WILL NEED:

- ♥ Cake
- ♥ Dark cooking chocolate
- ♥ Buttercream
- ♥ 15cm (6in) lollipop sticks
- ♥ Star plunger cutters
- ♥ Sugarpaste
- ♥ Gold edible lustre spray

1. Crumble the cake into a mixing bowl. Bind your cake crumb with buttercream at a ratio of 2:1 – two parts cake to one part binding.

2. Roll your mixture into balls of roughly 3cm–4cm (1⅛in–1½in) diameter (approximately 25g/1oz), put them on a sheet of baking paper on a tray, and place them in your freezer for 15 minutes, or your refrigerator for an hour or so, to firm up.

3. Use a lollipop stick to poke a hole half way into each ball. Pour a little melted chocolate into each hole and then insert your sticks. Freeze or refrigerate the cake pops again to harden the chocolate, which helps keep the sticks in place.

4. Get a big bowl full of melted chocolate and dip each cake pop in until fully coated. Shake off the excess chocolate and then place your cake pops in a cake pop stand.

5. Finally, roll out 1mm–2mm (³⁄₃₂in) thick sheets of sugarpaste and make some stars using your star plunger cutters; spray them gold with the lustre spray. Allow to dry and then attach them to your pops using a dab of chocolate and place in the refrigerator to dry. Drizzle your cake pops with melted white chocolate for added indulgence!

Elegant Mini Cakes

by Ruth Clemens

YOU WILL NEED:

- ♥ 6.5cm (2½in) mini cakes
- ♥ Buttercream
- ♥ 10cm (4in) cake card
- ♥ Purple sugarpaste
- ♥ White sugar florist paste (SFP)
- ♥ Purple royal icing
- ♥ No.2 piping nozzle
- ♥ Flower cutters
  Large, medium and small carnation
- ♥ Edible glue
- ♥ Ball tool and flower pad
- ♥ Purple edible lustre dust
- ♥ White holographic cake sparkles
- ♥ Purple ribbon

1. Roll out purple sugarpaste to 2mm–3mm (³/₃₂in–¹/₈in) thick to cover the cake card; secure in place using a light mist of water. Set aside.

2. Prepare your mini cake for covering by coating with a thin layer of buttercream.

3. Roll out the purple sugarpaste this time to a depth of 5mm (³/₁₆in) on a surface lightly dusted with icing sugar to prevent it from sticking. Use to cover your mini cake smoothing to a fine finish using a cake smoother. Position each cake in the centre of a covered cake card securing it with a dot of buttercream.

4. Roll out the white SFP very thinly to a 1mm–2mm (³/₃₂in) thickness. Cut out one large, four medium and four small carnations. Set them onto the flower pad and use the ball tool to thin the edges of the petals, pressing them in a circular motion.

5. Using the recesses of an empty egg tray create the three flowers for the cake. Beginning with the largest flower lay the following together securing each layer with a dab of edible glue:
Large flower: one large, two medium and one small.
Medium flower: two medium and one small.
Small flower: two small.
Allow to dry.

6. Fill a piping bag fitted with a no.2 nozzle with purple royal icing. Beginning at the base of the cake pipe swirly lines all over until the cake is completely covered. Set aside to dry.

7. Using the purple lustre dust with a dry paintbrush, dust the centres of the three flowers to create a subtle hint of colour.

8. Once the flowers have dried, position them onto the cake securing with a bulb of royal icing. Pipe small dots of purple royal icing to create the flower centres. Sprinkle on some white holographic cake sparkles for a touch of glitz! Trim the cake base with a purple ribbon.

Pansy Posy Cupcakes
by Prudence Rogers

YOU WILL NEED:

♥ Vanilla cupcakes baked in cupcake liners
Cath Kidston Green Polka Dot

♥ Vanilla buttercream

♥ Sugarpaste

♥ White royal icing

♥ Pansy flower and leaf cutters

♥ Edible black pen

♥ Red, orange and light green gel food colouring

1. Colour three small amounts of sugarpaste dark pink, orange and light green using the gel food colourings.

2. Roll out the dark pink and orange sugarpaste to 2mm (³/₃₂in) thick and use a pansy cutter to cut petals. Join four petals together using a little water to create a flower. Place into an empty egg box to create a cupped shape and leave to dry. Make four or five flowers for each cupcake.

3. Roll out the light green sugarpaste to 2mm (³/₃₂in) thick. Cut out eight or nine leaves for each cupcake using the leaf cutter. Use a blunt knife pressed lightly into the surface of the leaves to create the veins. Leave to dry.

4. Take the vanilla cupcakes baked in cupcake liners and, when cooled, pipe with a swirl of vanilla buttercream. Use white royal icing to pipe a small curved centre onto each flower.

5. Then use an edible black pen to create lines radiating from the middle. Stick your pansies onto the buttercream, alternating between pink and orange flowers. Leave small gaps between groups of flowers and intersperse with the leaves.

Christmas Tree Cakes

by Zoe Scott

YOU WILL NEED:

- ♥ Fruit cake mixture
- ♥ Six-cup king size muffin tin
- ♥ Red, green and gold cake glitter
  Holly Cupcake
- ♥ Apricot jam and marzipan
- ♥ Homemade royal icing (see step 3)

1. Grease the six-cup king size muffin tin, cut 12 strips of greaseproof paper 20cm (7⅞in) long, arrange in crosses in each hole of the tin. Pour in the fruit cake mixture and bake in a bain marie, until a skewer comes out clean; cool slightly then use the paper to remove.

2. Once cool, brush cakes with apricot jam, roll out the marzipan and cut four circles approximately 22cm (8⅝in) in diameter (use a side plate as a guide). Cut approximately a third out of each circle to make a cone of marzipan around the cakes, using the cut outs for the remaining two cakes.

3. Make the royal icing. Whisk three egg whites to soft peaks then gradually add 550g (2lb 4oz) icing sugar until stiff peaks form. Finally add a teaspoon of glycerine with some green food colouring. Using a small palette knife spread the icing over the cakes. Starting at the base dab and pull the palette knife to create peaks.

4. From the remaining marzipan cut six stars and roll lots of small balls for baubles.

5. Brush with jam, then sprinkle with the gold cake glitter. Sprinkle the trees with green cake glitter and then decorate with the stars and baubles.

6. For an extra touch, cut squares of cake and cover with marzipan and royal icing coloured with red and sprinkle with the red cake glitter to make presents for the bottom of the trees. Leave the finished cakes to dry overnight or up to two days, until firm.

Pink Daisy Cupcakes
by Ruth Clemens

YOU WILL NEED:

♥ Six cupcakes baked in white paper cases

♥ Buttercream

♥ Circular cookie cutter

♥ Sage, pink and pale pink sugarpaste

♥ White royal icing

♥ No.2 piping nozzle

♥ Flower cutters
  Large and small daisy plunger cutters and medium calyx cutter

1. Roll out the sage sugarpaste to 3mm (⅛in) thick and cut out round circles to fit the cupcake tops.

2. Coat the tops of the cupcakes with a thin layer of buttercream and place the sage green circles in position.

3. Add the white royal icing to a piping bag fitted with a no.2 piping nozzle. From the centre pipe four lines right up to the edge of the case, dividing the cupcake into quarters. Between each full length line pipe a shorter line to reach half way between the centre and the outside edge.

4. Now pipe a line between each full length and half length lines that reaches approximately three-quarters of the way to the outside edge. Pipe two dots following each short line. Finish all of the other piped lines with a bulb at the end of each. If your royal icing dots have peaks, dab them down gently with a damp paintbrush. Set the cupcakes aside to dry.

5. Roll out the pink sugarpaste paste to a thickness of 2mm (³⁄₃₂in) on a surface lightly dusted with icing sugar to prevent it from sticking. Cut out six large daisies. Repeat with the pale pink sugarpaste cutting out six small daisies. Cut out six medium calyx from the sage green sugarpaste.

6. Apply a dot of royal icing to the centre of the cupcake and place the calyx in position. Add another dot of royal icing to the centre of the calyx and add the large pink daisy. The small pale pink daisy is secured in the centre using a small dab of water applied to the back. Pipe small dots of royal icing to create the centres of the flowers using a damp paintbrush to flatten any peaks.

Celebration Mini Cakes

by Sue Ellis

YOU WILL NEED:

- ♥ Cake ingredients and brandy

- ♥ Apricot jam and marzipan

- ♥ Six 7.5cm (3in) diameter baking tins

- ♥ Cutters in a variety of shapes

- ♥ Mini cake boards

- ♥ White ready-roll fondant icing

- ♥ Ribbon

1. Make a fruit cake mix using the ingredients for a 20cm (8in) Christmas cake recipe. Line the baking tins with greaseproof paper and divide the cake mixture equally between them. Bake until golden brown on a low heat setting 140°C, 275°F, Gas Mark 1. Allow to cool.

2. Douse the cakes in brandy and leave them to mature. Two weeks before event, place each on a mini cake board, coat with warm apricot jam and cover with marzipan.

3. When you are ready to cover your cakes with the fondant icing, you will need to prepare them by brushing them lightly with boiled water so that the icing adheres to the marzipan.

4. Roll out the fondant icing to about 2mm (³⁄₃₂in) thick, lay it on top of the cake and use a smoother to gently smooth over the top and down around the sides. Trim off the excess icing and repeat until all cakes are covered and smooth.

5. Decorate the top of each cake with your own sugar decorations made from fondant icing. Use hearts and moulded flowers for Valentines day or weddings. Create stars for birthdays and for a festive Christmas theme use snowflake or holly cutters. All icing can be coloured using edible paste or dust and to add a sparkle, lustre dust can be used to brush gently on top. Just add ribbon to the cake base complete the right look for the occasion.

Frilly Flower Cupcakes

by Fiona Pearce

YOU WILL NEED:

- ♥ Cupcakes baked in black polka dot cupcake cases
- ♥ Garrett frill cutter set
- ♥ White flower paste
- ♥ Buttercream and pink sugarpaste
- ♥ Edible glue
- ♥ Decorative edge punch Martha Stewart doily lace
- ♥ A4 silver paper

1. Roll out some flower paste finely with a non-stick rolling pin. Use a garret frill cutter to cut out four ring-shaped pieces with scalloped edges. Roll a cocktail stick (toothpick) backwards and forwards on the scalloped edges to frill them. Cut each ring with a knife so that the frill can be opened out into a strip.

2. Arrange the first frilled strip into a circle, making sure the diameter of the circle is slightly smaller than the top of the cupcake.

3. Using a thin paintbrush, add a small amount of edible glue to the non-frilled edge of the circle and attach the next frilled strip in a circular motion. Continue this process until all frilled strips have been added and the hole in the centre of the circle is completely filled. You will need four frilly strips for each flower.

4. Use pieces of kitchen towel or a paper napkin to separate the frilly layers while they are drying.

5. Decorate the tops of your cakes with circles of pink sugarpaste. Once the flowers have dried, transfer each onto the top of a cupcake and attach with buttercream.

6. To make a cupcake wrapper, use scissors to cut a silver paper arc long enough to wrap around the cake. Use the edge punch along the longer side of the paper arc for a lace pattern. Wrap around the cupcake with the lace pattern at the top and secure with double-sided tape.

Mini Christmas Pudding Cakes

by Zoe Scott

YOU WILL NEED:

- ♥ Fruit cake mixture
- ♥ Six-cup king size muffin tin
- ♥ Holly cutter
- ♥ Red, gold and green cake glitter
  Holly Cupcake
- ♥ Homemade fondant icing
- ♥ Green and red sugarpaste

1. Grease the muffin tin, cut 12 strips of greaseproof paper 20cm (7⅞in) long, arrange in crosses in each hole of the tin. Pour in the fruit cake mixture and bake in a bain marie until a skewer comes out clean; cool slightly then use the paper to remove.

2. Roll out the green sugarpaste and cut out 12 holly leaves. Moisten slightly with a drop of water and sprinkle with green cake glitter.

3. Roll 18 balls of red sugarpaste, moisten slightly and sprinkle with red cake glitter.

4. Mix up fondant icing and dip each cake narrow end in up to half way and quickly turn back onto the wider base to allow the fondant to drip; sprinkle with gold cake glitter.

5. Add the holly leaves and berries on top of the fondant icing whilst still wet and leave to firm, then store in an airtight container until serving.

Button Blossom Cupcakes

by Ruth Clemens

YOU WILL NEED:

- ♥ Six cupcakes baked in white paper cases
- ♥ Buttercream
- ♥ Circular cookie cutter
- ♥ Purple and lime green sugarpaste
- ♥ Purple royal icing
- ♥ No.2 piping nozzle
- ♥ Flower cutters
  Small five-petal blossom cutter and small blossom plunger cutter

1. Roll out the lime green sugarpaste to 2mm (³⁄₃₂in) thick on a surface lightly dusted with icing sugar. Cut out six small five-petal blossoms and 24 small blossoms with the plunger cutter. Place the five-petal blossoms into the recesses of an empty egg box to help shape the petals. To create the buttons for the centres of the five-petal blossoms, roll out a little purple sugarpaste to 3mm (⅛in) thick.

2. Using the wide end of the no.2 piping nozzle cut out 6 circles. Make two indents in each button for the centre. Apply a dab of water to the centre of each blossom and place a button, securing with a light press.

3. Coat the tops of the cupcakes with a thin layer of buttercream and place on purple circles cut to fit from purple sugarpaste rolled out to 3mm (⅛in) thick.

4. Add the purple royal icing to a piping bag fitted with the no.2 nozzle. Secure the large blossom in position on the top of the cupcake using a dot of royal icing. Position the small blossoms across the tops of the cupcakes adhering with a little water applied to the back of each. Pipe small dots to the centre of each small blossom and then pipe small bulbs of royal icing for the polka dots, dabbing down any peaks with a damp paintbrush.

Party Hat Cupcakes

by Ruth Clemens

YOU WILL NEED:

- ♥ Six cupcakes
- ♥ White sugarpaste
- ♥ White sugar florist paste (SFP)
- ♥ Green, blue and purple gel paste colours
- ♥ Buttercream
- ♥ Fluted circle cutter 5.5cm (2¼in) diameter
- ♥ Round cutter 5mm (³⁄₁₆in) diameter
- ♥ Large open star piping nozzle
- ♥ Disposable piping bag

1. Knead together equal amounts of white sugarpaste and white SFP. Colour portions light green, blue and purple, leaving the remainder white. Roll out the light green paste to 2mm (³⁄₃₂in) thick. Cut out six fluted circles and set aside to dry.

2. Shape six cone-shaped hats 3cm (1⅛in) high by rolling white paste first into a ball, tapering the top and then flattening the base. Secure each hat onto the green discs using a little water.

3. Create the details for each hat in blue, purple and green. Roll a 7mm (⁹⁄₃₂in) ball for the top and secure with a dab of water. Roll a thin sausage 7cm (2¾in) long and wind around the base. Roll out a little paste to 1mm (¹⁄₁₆in) thick, cut out five dots and add around the side of the hat.

4. Roll out a little blue and purple paste very thinly. Use a roller cutter to cut strips 10cm (4in) long by 5mm (³⁄₁₆in) wide. Wind gently around a cocktail stick then slide off.

5. Add a purple and blue streamer to the side of the party hat. Fit the open star nozzle to a piping bag and fill with buttercream. Pipe swirls to the tops of each cupcake and place your cupcake toppers in position.

Balloon Mini Cake

by Ruth Clemens

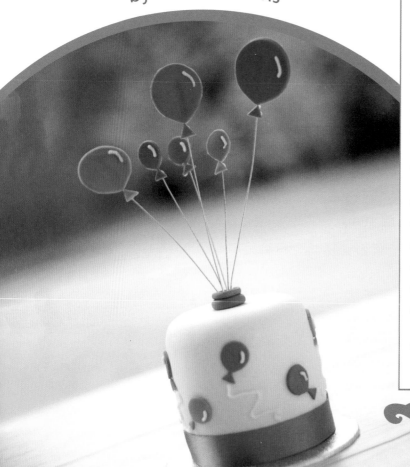

YOU WILL NEED:

- ♥ One 6.5cm (2½in) mini cake
- ♥ Buttercream
- ♥ 10cm (4in) diameter cake card
- ♥ White sugarpaste
- ♥ White sugar florist paste (SFP)
- ♥ Red, green and blue gel paste colours
- ♥ White royal icing
- ♥ Disposable piping bag
- ♥ No. 2 piping nozzle
- ♥ 24-gauge florists' wire
- ♥ Cake pick
- ♥ Medium and small rose petal cutters
- ♥ Bright blue ribbon

1. Prepare your mini cake for covering by applying a thin layer of buttercream. Roll out the white sugarpaste to 5mm (³⁄₁₆in) thick on a surface lightly dusted with icing sugar. Use the paste to cover the mini cake smoothing to a fine finish with a cake smoother.

2. Position the covered cake in the centre of the cake card and secure with a dot of buttercream. Trim the base of the cake with bright blue ribbon secured at the back with a pearl-headed pin.

3. Knead together equal amounts of white sugarpaste and SFP. Colour one third red, one third blue and one third green. Roll out one colour at a time to 2mm (³⁄₃₂in) thick. Using the medium rose petal cutter, cut out one of each colour for the large balloons. Using the small petal cutter, cut out four of each colour for the small balloons. Using a sharp knife cut out small triangles in each colour to match the body of the balloons. Set aside to dry.

4. When the balloon pieces have dried out, begin the assembly. Cut six pieces of florists' wire approximately 15cm (6in) long. Fit a piping bag with a no. 2 piping nozzle and fill with white royal icing. Secure one piece of wire along the back of one medium balloon and one small balloon in each colour using the royal icing. Allow the icing to dry.

5. Once the icing has fully dried, turn over each balloon and secure the small triangle in place for the balloon tail, again using a bulb of royal icing. Add a small reflection mark to the front of each balloon.

Leave to allow the icing to dry fully.

6. Secure the remaining balloons in a random colour pattern around the side of the cake using royal icing. Pipe white ribbon tails and a small reflection mark for each.

7. Insert the cake pick into the centre of the top of the cake. Gather together the wired balloons and arrange in a spray. Secure the ends of the wires together by using the a piece of wire to wind around them, and insert into the cake pick.

8. Roll two short thin sausages of red and blue paste and position around the top of the cake pick, securing in place with a light brush of water.

Flower Basket Cake

by Ruth Clemens

YOU WILL NEED:

♥ One 6.5cm (2½in) mini cake

♥ Buttercream

♥ 7.5cm (3in) square cake card

♥ White sugarpaste

♥ White sugar florist paste (SFP)

♥ Red, green and brown gel paste colours

♥ White royal icing

♥ Disposable piping bag

♥ Circle cutter 5cm (2in) diameter

♥ Red ribbon

1. Apply a thin buttercream layer to the cake. Roll out the white sugarpaste to 5mm (³⁄₁₆in) thick and cover the cake smoothing to a fine finish. Use a dot of buttercream to secure the cake to the centre of the cake card; trim with red ribbon.

2. Knead together equal amounts or white sugarpaste and SFP; divide into four equal parts. Leave one quarter white; colour the others red, green and brown. Roll out brown paste to 2mm (³⁄₃₂in) thick, cut a circle, and place over a rolling pin to make a basket shape.

3. For leaves, pinch small green paste balls into teardrop shapes. Gently flatten and score a line down the centre. Make 12, each 1cm (³⁄₈in) long. For flowers, roll red and white thin paste sausages 2cm (¾in) long. Flatten one long edge and roll up from the end. Trim excess at base. Make four red and six white. Cut a brown paste basket handle measuring 6mm x 6cm (¼in x 2³⁄₈in); secure to the inside of the basket. Line the edge with leaves and fill with flowers attached with a little piped royal icing. Make tiny leaves to fill in between. Attach the basket to the mini cake with a little royal icing.

Cookie Bouquet

by Prudence Rogers

YOU WILL NEED:

- ♥ Heart-shaped cookie tin
- ♥ Batch of cookie dough
- ♥ Oven-proof cookie sticks
- ♥ Vegetable oil spray
- ♥ Dark cocoa and white candy melts
- ♥ Chocolate transfer sheets
- ♥ White chocolate and mini red heart sprinkles
- ♥ Patterned ribbons

1. Lightly spray the tin with vegetable oil spray. Pat cookie dough into each heart shape until about 3mm (⅛in) below the edge. Insert cookie sticks in the indentations up to the marker line (about 5cm/2in). Bake at 180°C/350°F for about 15 minutes until firm to touch and golden brown. Allow to cool.

2. Prepare the candy melts following the manufacturer's instructions. Cover the cookies by pouring the candy melts all over; tap off the excess and place onto greaseproof paper.

3. Before the chocolate sets, cut a piece of chocolate transfer sheet to roughly the same size as the cookie and lay on top. Press down gently all over and set aside. When the chocolate has set hard, peel off the backing sheet, leaving the design on the cookie. For a variation, before the chocolate sets, sprinkle white chocolate flakes or red heart sprinkles over the cookie. Leave to set. This looks best if there is a good contrast.

4. Cut lengths of patterned ribbons to approx 30cm (12in). Tie the ribbons around the cookie sticks at the base of the hearts. Trim the ends of the ribbon at an angle with scissors.

Cupcake Love

by Sarah Joyce

YOU WILL NEED:

- ♥ Chocolate cupcake mixture
- ♥ Raspberries and raspberry coulis syrup
- ♥ Chocolate buttercream icing
- ♥ 30g (1oz) white chocolate
- ♥ Seven red cupcake wrappers
- ♥ White writer icing tube
- ♥ No. 2 piping nozzle
- ♥ Disposable piping bags

1. Before baking the chocolate cupcakes push a raspberry into each. Once baked, brush the top of the warm cupcakes with strained raspberry coulis syrup. When completely cooled, decorate.

2. Fill a piping bag, fitted with a no. 2 piping nozzle, with the chocolate buttercream icing.

3. Starting from the centre of each cupcake, pipe a swirl to the edge to give a rose effect.

4. To make the chocolate heart decorations, melt the white chocolate in a plastic bowl by microwaving on medium power for 10-second bursts, stirring between each.

5. Use the melted chocolate to fill a piping bag fitted with PME supatube no. 2 nozzle and pipe heart shapes onto baking paper. Leave to set for 2 hours at room temperature. Once the chocolate hearts have dried completely, lift carefully and place one on the top of each cupcake. Place a fresh raspberry in the centre of each heart, and finish the cupcakes with the red wrappers.

Bird's Nest Cupcakes

by James Brooks

YOU WILL NEED:

- ♥ One batch of chocolate cupcakes
- ♥ One batch of chocolate buttercream
- ♥ Disposable piping bag
- ♥ Large star piping nozzle size 13
- ♥ White Mexican modelling paste
- ♥ Yellow, orange and black paste colours
- ♥ Mini chocolate eggs

1. Take the chocolate buttercream and spoon it into a disposable piping bag fitted with a large star piping nozzle. To make the nest, pipe a ring of buttercream around the outside edge of each cupcake leaving the centre clear.

2. Now make the chicks. Colour some of the modelling paste yellow and some orange. Take a little yellow paste and roll it into a small ball to make the chick's body.

3. Take a small amount of orange paste and roll it into two cone shapes to make a beak. Stick the beak to the chick's body using a dab of water. Make as many chicks as you have cupcakes.

4. To complete the modelling paste chicks dip a cocktail stick in the black paste colour and use it to carefully dab two eyes onto each chick's face. Set the chicks aside until completely dry.

5. Place one chick and a mini chocolate egg inside the chocolate 'nest' on top of each cupcake to finish.

Bunny Biscuits

by Ruth Clemens

YOU WILL NEED:

- ♥ Six circular biscuits
- ♥ White sugarpaste
- ♥ White sugar florist paste (SFP)
- ♥ Brown, green and blue gel paste colours
- ♥ Royal icing
- ♥ Black icing pen
- ♥ Disposable piping bags
- ♥ No. 1, 2 and 3 piping nozzles
- ♥ Fluted circle cutter 5.5cm (2¼in) diameter

1. Knead together equal amounts of white sugarpaste and white SFP. Colour the paste a pale blue using gel paste colouring. Roll out the blue paste to 2mm (³⁄₃₂in) thick. Cut out six fluted circles and set aside to dry. Once dry, prepare the royal icing. Colour one third brown and one third green. Put the green royal icing in a piping bag fitted with a no. 1 nozzle and the remaining white in a bag fitted with a no. 2 nozzle. Add a drop of water to loosen the brown royal icing and add to a piping bag fitted with a no. 3 nozzle.

2. Decorate the circles: allow each piped part to dry slightly before adding the next to avoid bleeding.

For the feet: pipe two brown teardrops, one third of the way up.

For the body: pipe a 1.5cm (⅝in) bulb just above the feet.

For the head: pipe a 1cm (⅜in) bulb.

For the ears: pipe two teardrops, flopping one over slightly.

For the grass: use green either side.

For the whiskers: use black icing pen to draw onto either side of the head.

For the bobtail: add a small bulb of white to base of body.

3. Allow the royal icing to dry completely before securing each disc to the top of each biscuit using a light brush of water.

Daisy Button Cupcakes

by Fiona Pearce

YOU WILL NEED:

- ♥ One batch of vanilla cupcakes
- ♥ White and pink sugar florist paste (SFP)
- ♥ White and pale green sugarpaste
- ♥ Circle, large daisy and small leaf plunger cutters
- ♥ Silicone button mould
- ♥ Edible glue

1. Roll out some white SFP finely on a non-stick surface. Use the daisy cutter to cut out three flowers for each cupcake.

2. Place the flowers into an empty egg carton to mould them into their distinctive cupped shape. Leave the flowers to dry so that they hold their shape.

3. Roll out some green sugarpaste to 2mm (³/₃₂in) thick. Use the small leaf plunger cutter to cut out three leaves for each cupcake, pushing the plunger down to imprint veins into the leaf. Pinch the base of each leaf into a 'V' shape.

4. Press some pink SFP into a silicone button mould to make three buttons for each cupcake.

5. Attach the buttons into the centre of each flower using edible glue applied with a fine paintbrush.Cover the top of each cupcake with a circle of white sugarpaste that has been rolled out to 3mm (¹/₈in) thick. Attach the flowers and the leaves to the centre of the cupcakes using edible glue.

Team Colour Cakes

by Prudence Rogers

YOU WILL NEED:

♥ One batch of vanilla mini cake sponges and one batch of buttercream icing

♥ 10cm (4in) diameter cake cards

♥ White sugarpaste and green food colouring

♥ Red, black and brown gel paste colours

♥ No. 233 grass piping nozzle

1. Colour a portion of sugarpaste green, roll out thinly; use to cover the cake cards with a drop of water.

2. For the scarf design cover the mini cake evenly with buttercream icing and chill to firm. Roll out white sugarpaste to 5mm (³⁄₁₆in) thick and cover the cake, working the icing around the sides with your hands; trim away excess. Use a dab of royal icing to stick the cake to the card.

3. Cut out six hexagons from 3mm (1¹⁄₈in) thick black sugarpaste; apply in an evenly spaced pattern to the cake top with a little water. Make red and white sugarpaste sausages 5cm (2in) long by 1.5cm (⁵⁄₈in) wide. Arrange next to each other so they are touching, alternating the colours. Roll out to 5mm (³⁄₁₆in) thick so the colours join to make stripes. Cut a rectangle 3mm (¹⁄₈in) taller than the cake height, and 5cm (2in) less than the cake's circumference.

4. Roll red/blue and white sugarpaste balls; add to the scarf end with water. Squeeze more sugarpaste through a sugarcraft extruder gun for tassels. Bunch up at one end and join to the balls.

5. For the sports field design pipe green buttercream all over the cake. Roll a brown sugarpaste rugby ball, indent seams and use white sugarpaste for the stitching.

Hexagon Template

Lacy Heart Cupcakes
by Fiona Pearce

YOU WILL NEED:

- ♥ One batch of cupcakes
- ♥ White and pale pink sugarpaste
- ♥ White royal icing
- ♥ Disposable piping bag
- ♥ No. 2 piping nozzle
- ♥ Quilting tool
- ♥ Small blossom plunger cutter
- ♥ Circle cutter
- ♥ Edible glue
- ♥ Lacy cupcake wrappers
- ♥ Foam mat
- ♥ Ball modelling tool

1. Roll out the white sugarpaste to 3mm (⅛in) thick. Use the circle cutter to cut circles from it. Use the palm of your hand to smooth each circle into position on top of the cakes; use the quilting tool to imprint the criss-cross pattern.

2. Roll out the pink sugarpaste to 2mm (³⁄₃₂in) thick. Use the blossom plunger cutter to cut 16 small blossoms for each cupcake.

3. Place the small pale pink blossoms onto a foam mat. Gently press the small end of a ball modelling tool into the centre of the blossoms to give each of them a lovely cupped shape.

4. Arrange the cupped blossoms on top of each cupcake to form a heart shape, using edible glue applied with a fine paintbrush to hold them in place.

5. Pipe a small dot of white royal icing into the centre of each blossom using a piping bag fitted with a no. 2 nozzle. Place the cupcakes into the cupcake wrappers to finish.

Bride and Groom Cakes
by James Brooks

YOU WILL NEED:

- ♥ Half batch vanilla cupcakes
- ♥ Half batch chocolate cupcakes
- ♥ One batch buttercream
- ♥ White Mexican modelling paste
- ♥ Pink and black paste colours
- ♥ Pink candy food dust
- ♥ Cake push pop holders
- ♥ Disposable piping bag

1. Assemble the push pops. Colour buttercream pink, spoon into the piping bag and snip off the end. For the bride push pops, cut two circles from vanilla cupcakes using a push pop tube and top each with a simple swirl of pink buttercream. Repeat for the groom push pops using the chocolate cupcakes.

2. To make the top hat: add black paste colour to white modelling paste to make silver-grey. Roll out a little and use a push pop tube to cut a circle for the hat base.

3. Roll out a paste sausage smaller than the circle; cut off a 2.5cm (1in) segment, ensuring both ends remain perfectly flat. Stick to the circle with a dab of water; set aside to dry. Complete the top hat by adding a thin ribbon of pink-coloured modelling paste around the base of the hat.

4. To make the rose, cut out four circles from rolled out white modelling paste. Smooth the top edge of each circle with your thumb to form the edges of the petals.

5. Roll one petal closed, with the thin edge at the top, to form the centre of the rose. Roll the three remaining petals around this. Set aside to dry, then place the top hats and roses on top of the push pops.

Baby's Onesie Cookies

by Fiona Pearce

1. Roll out the cookie dough to 5mm (³⁄₁₆in) and use a small knife to cut out the cookies into the bodysuit shape using the onesie template as a guide. Bake according to your recipe, then leave to cool completely before decorating.

2. Equally divide the royal icing into two bowls. Leaving one half white, colour the other half with blue or pink food colouring.

3. Using half of each batch of royal icing, fill disposable piping bags fitted with no. 2 piping nozzle. Add a few drops of water to the remaining royal icing and mix until a runny consistency is achieved. Fill squeeze bottles with the runny royal icing. Pipe royal icing from the piping bag around the edge of each cookie. Fill the piped outline with the runny royal icing from the squeeze bottle, using a cocktail stick to guide the icing into empty spaces or to pop any air bubbles.

4. Once each cookie is filled, squeeze little dots of another colour of the runny royal icing onto the wet icing to achieve the polka dot effect.

5. Leave the cookies to dry for 3–4 hours before piping the garment details on the top of the cookies.

Baby's Onesie Cookie Template

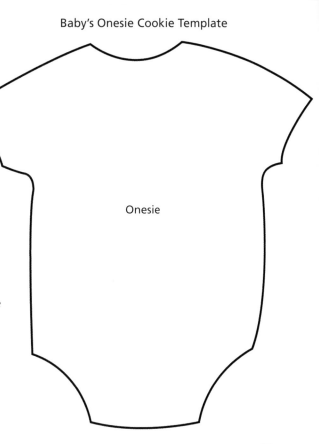

Onesie

Flower Cupcakes
by Kate Kerly

YOU WILL NEED:

- ♥ Batch of 12 cupcakes
- ♥ White sugarpaste
- ♥ Pink and blue food colouring
- ♥ White sugar pearls
- ♥ Buttercream
- ♥ Edible silver glitter
- ♥ Patterned scroll roller
- ♥ Flower cutter
- ♥ Disposable piping bag
- ♥ Star piping nozzle

1. Take some of the white sugarpaste and colour it blue or pink with a few drops of food colouring. Roll out the coloured paste to 5mm (³⁄₁₆in) thick. Roll the scroll roller over the sugarpaste to indent the pattern, and use the flower cutter to cut out 12 flowers. Set aside to harden.

2. Once the flowers have dried completely, add white sugar pearls to the centres using a dot of buttercream, then leave to dry. Fill a piping bag fitted with a large star nozzle with buttercream. Pipe large swirls on top of each cupcake. Place a flower on top of the buttercream.

3. To finish the cupcakes dust each one with edible silver glitter and dot a few of the white sugar pearls around the edges.

Ghostly Cupcakes
by Fiona Pearce

YOU WILL NEED:

- ♥ Circular biscuits
  (7.5cm/3in diameter)

- ♥ White, blue, purple
  and pink sugarpaste

- ♥ Pink, purple, golden yellow
  and black royal icing

- ♥ Fluted cookie cutter and
  small round cutter

- ♥ Petal cutters
  Large, small and extra
  small rose petal

1. Cover the top of each cupcake with a thin layer of buttercream. Stack two marshmallows on top of the centre of each cupcake, using buttercream to stick them together. Add a little bit of buttercream on the top marshmallow to hold the sugarpaste covering in place.

2. Use a non-stick rolling pin to roll out some of the white sugarpaste in a rough circle shape approximately 3mm (⅛in) thick and about four times the cupcake diameter. Gently drape the sugarpaste over the top of the marshmallows to cover the whole cupcake and case.

3. Use a small knife to trim away any excess sugarpaste from around the base of the cupcake. Fill a piping bag fitted with the no. 2 piping nozzle with black royal icing and use to pipe eyes and a mouth onto each ghost. Allow the royal icing to dry before serving.

Pumpkin Cupcakes

by Ruth Clemens

YOU WILL NEED:

- ♥ One batch cupcakes baked in orange and black cases
- ♥ White sugarpaste
- ♥ White sugar florist paste (SFP)
- ♥ Black, orange and green gel paste colours
- ♥ Buttercream
- ♥ Royal icing
- ♥ Fluted circle cutter 5.5cm (2¼in) diameter and ivy leaf cutter
- ♥ Large open star piping nozzle
- ♥ Disposable piping bag

1. Knead together equal amounts of white sugarpaste and SFP, and colour portions orange, green and black. Roll out black and orange pastes to 2mm (³⁄₃₂in) thick. Cut out three fluted circles from each colour and set aside to dry.

2. Make three pumpkins: roll a 2.5cm (1in) orange paste ball; flatten the base slightly. Use a cocktail stick to mark vertical lines on the sides.

3. Cut out three leaves from thinly rolled out green paste. Secure to the pumpkin tops with a dab of water. Make a hole in the top of the pumpkin through the leaf to insert the stalk rolled from a tiny green paste sausage with tapered end.

4. Secure each pumpkin to a black disc. Cut tendrils from long thin green paste strips wound around a cocktail stick and attach.

5. Fill a piping bag fitted with an large open star nozzle with buttercream and pipe swirls onto each cupcake. Place the cupcake toppers in position on top.

Scary Cookie Lollies

by Ruth Clemens

YOU WILL NEED:

- ♥ Six Halloween-shaped cookies baked on lolly sticks

- ♥ White sugarpaste

- ♥ Black, orange and green gel paste colours

- ♥ Royal icing

- ♥ Bat, ghost and pumpkin cookie cutters

- ♥ Disposable piping bags

- ♥ No. 2 piping nozzles

- ♥ White disc sprinkles

1. Divide the white sugarpaste into thirds and colour two of the portions orange and black. Roll out each sugarpaste portion to 3mm (⅛in) thick and cut out using the corresponding cookie cutter (see photograph).

2. Use the cut out sugarpaste shapes to cover the relevant cookies and secure using a light brush of water.

3. Colour portions of the royal icing green, orange and black, keeping one portion white. Fill piping bags fitted with the no. 2 nozzles and pipe the outlines of the cookies using the corresponding colour.

4. Now add the fine detail. For the pumpkin cookies, pipe lines of orange to define the pumpkin's shape, then add a leafy top using the green royal icing. For the bat cookies, pipe on two small bulbs in black for the eyes. For the ghost cookies, pipe two small bulbs of royal icing to secure the two white disc sprinkle eyes, then pipe small bulbs of black for the pupils.

Mini Gingerbread House

by Fiona Pearce

YOU WILL NEED:

- ♥ One batch of gingerbread dough
- ♥ White royal icing
- ♥ Red sugarpaste
- ♥ Small heart cutter
- ♥ Disposable piping bag
- ♥ No. 2 piping nozzle

1. Use the templates to cut the gingerbread house pieces (front/back, roof and side) from card.

2. Roll out the gingerbread dough to 5mm (³⁄₁₆in). Use the card templates to cut two of each shape from the dough for each house to be made. Using a small knife, score windows into the house sides before baking gingerbread according to the recipe.

3. Allow the gingerbread pieces to cool before assembling and decorating. Fill piping bag fitted with a no. 2 nozzle with stiff peak white royal icing and use to attach the house front, back and sides where the surfaces join.

4. Attach the roof, then pipe a row of dots down the centre of the roof and under the eaves for decoration.

5. Decorate the roof with royal icing patterns. Alternatively, if you are using the gingerbread house as a place card, pipe on a name.

6. Roll out the red sugarpaste to 3mm (⅛in) thick. Use the small heart cutter to cut out two hearts for each house. Attach the hearts with a small dot of royal icing to the gable ends. Allow the royal icing to dry completely.

Mini Gingerbread House Templates

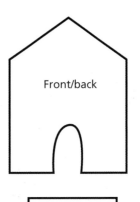

Front/back

Roof

Side

Santa Cookie Lollies

by Ruth Clemens

YOU WILL NEED:

- ♥ Six circular cookies baked on lolly sticks
- ♥ White sugarpaste
- ♥ Red and peach gel paste colours
- ♥ White royal icing
- ♥ Black icing pen
- ♥ Circular cookie cutter 8cm (3⅛in) diameter
- ♥ Disposable piping bag
- ♥ Small open star piping nozzle
- ♥ Small embossing rolling pin

1. Colour portions of white sugarpaste red and peach. Roll out the peach sugarpaste to 3mm (⅛in) thick and cut out six circles to cover the cookies, securing in place with a light brush of water.

2. Roll out red sugarpaste 3mm (⅛in) thick and cut out six circles; cut away the bottom two-thirds of each circle with the cutter to create hats. Secure the hats to the cookies. Use the wrong end of the piping nozzle to mark Santa's smile.

3. Roll out white sugarpaste to 2mm (³⁄₃₂in) thick, then go over it with a small embossing rolling pin to imprint a pattern. Cut out 10 circles, then use the cutter to cut away the top one-third from six of the circles to create the beard.

4. Dividing the remaining four circles into thirds, cut away the outside edge to create the moustache pieces. Secure the beard then the moustache onto Santa's face.

5. Make six small peach sugarpaste ball noses and secure each in place. Using a piping bag fitted with the small open star piping nozzle, pipe a royal icing fur trim to the hat. Add Santa's eyes with the black icing pen.

Techniques

This section will be very useful for those new to sugarcraft. It includes some basic cake and cookie recipes, and has everything you need to know about colouring and modelling with sugarpaste to create, sweet, stunning centrepieces for any party table. Whether you are planning on making the Cocktail Cookies for an elegant drinks party, the Swirl Cupcakes for a wedding reception, or the Hedgehog Cake for a child's birthday party, there are a few basics – equipment and recipes – that you can't do without.

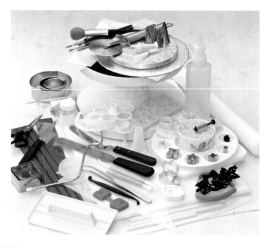

Baking essentials

♥ **Large electric mixer** – For making cakes, buttercream and royal icing.

♥ **Kitchen scales** – For weighing out ingredients.

♥ **Measuring spoons** – For small quantities.

♥ **Mixing bowls** – For mixing ingredients.

♥ **Spatulas** – For mixing and gently folding together cake mixes.

♥ **Cake tins** – For baking cakes.

♥ **Bun tray/ muffin tray** – For baking cupcakes.

♥ **Baking trays** – For baking cookies.

♥ **Wire racks** – For cooling cakes.

Vanilla cookies

Makes 10–15 large cookies or 25–30 medium cookies

Cookies are great fun to make for just about any occasion. You can cut out any shapes from the cookie dough and decorate them however you like. This dough can be made up to two weeks ahead or stored in the freezer until ready to use.

♥ 250g (9oz) unsalted butter

♥ 250g (9oz) caster (superfine) sugar

♥ 1–2 medium eggs

♥ 1 teaspoon vanilla extract

♥ 500g (1lb 2oz) plain (all-purpose) flour

For different flavour variations it is easy to modify the basic cookie recipe.
For chocolate cookies substitute 50g (1¾oz) flour with cocoa powder (unsweetened cocoa).
For citrus cookies add the finely grated zest of one lemon or orange.
For almond cookies replace the vanilla extract with 1 teaspoon almond extract.

1. Beat the butter and sugar together until creamy and quite fluffy. Add the eggs and vanilla extract and mix until they are well combined.

2. Sift the flour, add to the bowl and mix until all the ingredients just come together. You may need to do this in two stages – do not over-mix.

3. Tip the dough into a container lined with clingfilm (plastic wrap) and press down firmly. Cover with clingfilm and refrigerate for at least 30 minutes.

4. On a work surface lightly dusted with flour, roll out the cookie dough to about 4mm (1/8in) thick. Sprinkle a little extra flour on top of the dough as you roll to prevent it from sticking to the rolling pin.

5. Cut out your shapes using your cutters. Place on baking trays lined with greaseproof (wax) paper and return to the fridge to rest for at least 30 minutes.

6. Bake the cookies in a preheated oven at 180°C/350°F/Gas Mark 4 for about 10 minutes, depending on their size, or until they are golden brown. Leave them to cool completely before storing them in an airtight container until you are ready to decorate them.

Vanilla cupcakes

Makes 12

Elegant and delicious, this recipe for classic vanilla cupcakes is sure to please any hungry cake fan. Why not try swapping the vanilla extract for lemon or orange flavouring for a completely different effect?

- ♥ 125g (4½oz) unsalted (sweet) butter or margarine
- ♥ 125g (4½oz) caster (superfine) sugar
- ♥ 125g (4½oz) self-raising (-rising) flour
- ♥ 2 large eggs
- ♥ 2 tbsp milk
- ♥ ½ tsp vanilla extract

1. Pre-heat the oven to 180°C/350°F or Gas Mark 4.

2. Cut the butter into small cubes, place in a bowl and beat until smooth.

3. Gradually add the sugar, creaming it together with the butter until the mixture goes pale.

4. Beat in the eggs, a little at a time, then add the milk and vanilla extract and mix together using an electric whisk or freestanding electric mixer.

5. Fold in the flour carefully with a large metal spoon, mixing all the ingredients together until just combined. Don't over mix as it may prevent your cupcakes from rising properly.

6. Spoon the cupcake mixture into cupcake cases, filling them approximately two thirds full. Alternatively, use a piping bag to pipe the mixture into cases.

7. Place your filled cupcake cases into a cupcake or small muffin tin (pan) and bake in a pre-heated oven for 15–20 minutes. Keep an eye on your cupcakes to ensure they do not burn. They will be spongy but firm when baked, with a light golden top, and a skewer or clean knife inserted into the centre should come out clean.

8. Remove the tin (pan) from the oven and place away from the heat for the cupcakes to cool for 10 minutes. When cool, turn the cupcakes out onto a wire rack to cool completely before decorating.

Tip: Ensure your butter and eggs are at room temperature before you begin.

Chocolate cupcakes

Makes 12

Gorgeous, indulgent, decadent chocolate! Add chocolate chips or rough-cut chunks of chocolate bar for double chocolate cupcakes.

- ♥ 125g (4½oz) unsalted (sweet) butter or margarine
- ♥ 125g (4½oz) caster (superfine) sugar
- ♥ 100g (3½oz) self-raising (-rising) flour
- ♥ 25g (¾oz) cocoa powder(unsweetened cocoa)
- ♥ 2 large eggs
- ♥ 2 tbsp milk

1. Pre-heat the oven to 180°C/350°F or Gas Mark 4.

2. Cut the butter into small cubes, place in a bowl and beat until smooth.

3. Gradually add the sugar, creaming it together with the butter until the mixture goes pale.

4. Beat in the eggs, a little at a time, then add the milk and mix together using an electric whisk or freestanding electric mixer.

5. Fold in the flour and the cocoa carefully with a large metal spoon, mixing all the ingredients together until just combined. Don't over mix as it may prevent your cupcakes from rising properly.

6. Spoon the cupcake mixture into cupcake cases, filling them approximately two thirds full. Alternatively, use a piping bag to pipe the mixture into cases.

7. Place your filled cupcake cases into a cupcake or small muffin tin (pan) and bake in a pre-heated oven for 15–20 minutes. Keep an eye on your cupcakes to ensure they do not burn. They will be spongy but firm when baked, and a skewer or clean knife inserted into the centre should come out clean.

8. Remove the tin (pan) from the oven and place away from the heat for the cupcakes to cool for 10 minutes. When cool, turn the cupcakes out onto a wire rack to cool completely before decorating.

Tip: For extra chocolate why not add some chocolate chips to the mixture at the same time as adding the flour and cocoa?

Vanilla sponge cake

18cm (7in) round cake

This recipe is a great base for the Flower Basket, Balloon and Team Colour mini cake projects.

♥ 180g (6¼oz) unsalted (sweet) butter or margarine

♥ 180g (6¼oz) caster (superfine) sugar

♥ 180g (6¼oz) self-raising (-rising) flour

♥ 25g (¾oz) cocoa powder (unsweetened cocoa)

♥ 3 large eggs

♥ 1 tsp baking powder

♥ 1½ tsp vanilla extract

1. Pre-heat the oven to 180°C/350°F or Gas Mark 4.

2. Cut the butter into small cubes, place in a bowl and beat until smooth.

3. Cream the sugar together with the eggs, vanilla extract and butter using an electric whisk or freestanding electric mixer.

4. Fold in the flour and baking powder carefully with a large metal spoon, mixing all the ingredients together until just combined.

5. Spoon the mixture into a pre-lined baking tin (pan) and smooth the surface with a spatula to ensure a level finish.

6. Bake in a pre-heated oven for about 25–30 minutes, or until well risen. When the cake feels firm to the touch and has a light golden surface, test the bake by inserting a skewer or clean knife into the centre – if it comes out clean the centre of the cake is baked.

7. Remove the tin (pan) from the oven and place away from the heat to cool for at least 10 minutes. When cool, turn the cake out onto a wire rack to cool completely before decorating.

Classic chocolate cake

13cm (5in) round cake / 20cm (8in) round cake

This recipe is really quick and easy to make and has a lovely light texture. Although the method is the same for both the 13cm (5in) and 20cm (8in) round cakes, the quantities for the ingredients will obviously differ.

The ingredients for the 13cm (5in) round cake can be used to make 10–12 cupcakes. Place your cupcake cases in a bun tray (muffin pan) and fill them half to two-thirds only.

you will need (for the 13cm/5in round cake) …

♥ 170g (6oz) plain (all purpose) flour

♥ 30g (1oz) cocoa powder (unsweetened cocoa)

♥ 1½ teaspoons baking powder

♥ 150g (5½oz) unsalted butter

♥ 130g (4½oz) caster (superfine) sugar

♥ 2½ large eggs

♥ 100ml (3½fl oz) full-fat (whole) milk

you will need (for the 20cm/8in round cake) …

♥ 365g (12½oz) plain (all purpose) flour

♥ 65g (2¼oz) cocoa powder (unsweetened cocoa)

♥ 3¼ teaspoons baking powder

♥ 325g (11½oz) unsalted butter

♥ 285g (10oz) caster (superfine) sugar

♥ 5 large eggs

♥ 220ml (8fl oz) full-fat (whole) milk

1. Preheat your oven to 160°C/325°F/ Gas Mark 3, and grease and line your tins.

2. Sift the flour, cocoa powder and baking powder together.

3. Beat the butter and sugar together until light and fluffy. Crack your eggs into a separate bowl. Add the eggs to the mixture gradually, beating well between each addition.

4. Add half the dry ingredients and mix until just combined before adding half the milk. Repeat with the remaining ingredients. Mix until the mixture starts to come together; finish mixing with a spatula and spoon into your prepared tins.

5. Bake in the oven until a skewer inserted into the centre of your cakes comes out clean. Check smaller cakes after 20 minutes and larger cakes after 40 minutes.

6. Leave to cool, then wrap the cakes well in clingfilm and refrigerate until ready to use.

Fruit cake

20cm (8in) round cake

Use this simple fruit cake recipe for the Mini Christmas Pudding and Christmas Tree Cakes project for a really authentic festive taste.

♥ 500g (1lb 1½oz) mixed dried fruit

♥ 50g (1¾oz) mixed (candied) peel

♥ 75ml (5 tbsp) sherry

♥ 100g (3½oz) butter

♥ 100g (3½oz) brown sugar

♥ 2 medium eggs

♥ Zest and juice of one large orange

♥ 225g (8oz) plain (all-purpose) flour

♥ A pinch (each) of mixed spice, cinnamon, salt and nutmeg

1. Soak the fruit and mixed (candied) peel overnight in the sherry.

2. Pre-heat the oven to 140°C/275°F or Gas Mark 1.

3. Cream the butter and sugar together in a bowl until pale.

4. Sift in the flour and spices then add the egg, orange juice and zest, and soaked fruit and liquid.

5. Line the base and sides of a tin (pan) with baking parchment and place in a bain marie. Bake for approximately one hour.

6. Check the cake is cooked through by inserting a skewer into the centre. Cover the tin (pan) with foil and allow it to cool for 10–20 minutes. Turn out and place on a wire rack to cool completely before decorating.

Gingerbread

Makes 10–12 medium gingerbread men

Tasty gingerbread dough, perfect for the Mini Gingerbread House project.

♥ 350g (12oz) plain (all-purpose) flour

♥ 125g (4½oz) unsalted (sweet) butter

♥ 175g (6oz) brown sugar

♥ 1 large egg

♥ 1 tsp bicarbonate of soda (baking soda)

♥ 3 tsp ground ginger

♥ 4 tbsp golden syrup (corn syrup)

1. Pre-heat the oven to 180°C/350°F or Gas Mark 4.

2. Sift the flour, ground ginger and soda together into a large mixing bowl.

3. Cut the butter into small cubes and add it to the mix, blending it until it takes on a breadcrumb appearance. Stir the sugar into the mix gradually.

4. Beat the egg and syrup together using an electric hand mixer and then add to the rest of the ingredients, mixing thoroughly.

5. Tip the dough out onto a lightly floured surface, knead until smooth and then roll out to your desired thickness.

6. Use cookie cutters or templates to cut shapes out of the dough and place on a lined baking tray leaving a little room between each shape.

7. Bake in a pre-heated oven for 12–15 minutes. Leave to cool on the tray for 10 minutes afterwards, then place the shapes on a wire rack to cool completely.

Baking mini cakes

These versatile treats are quite easy to make and really fun to decorate. You can use a specialist mini cake tin (pan) to create a large batch of cakes if you have one, but it's generally simpler to cut mini cake rounds out of a sheet cake.

1. Using any cake recipe, such as the Vanilla Sponge Cake recipe, make up a large batch of cake mix and bake it in a square or rectangular sheet cake tin (pan), at least 5cm (2in) in height.

2. Once the cake has cooled, chill it for several hours to firm it up and then begin cutting mini cake rounds from the cake using a mini cake cutter or other circular cutter.

3. Stack 2–3 rounds to reach your desired height, filling each layer with buttercream and jam (or any other tasty filling).

4. Once assembled, crumb-coat the outer surface of the mini cake with buttercream and then chill, ready to be decorated.

Buttercream

Buttercream can be stored in an airtight container until required. Use it to sandwich cakes together or to coat them before covering with sugarpaste.

you will need (to make one quantity) …

♥ 110g (3¾oz) unsalted butter

♥ 350g (12oz) icing (confectioners') sugar

1. Place the butter in a bowl and beat until the mixture is light and fluffy.

2. Sift in the icing sugar and continue to beat until the mixture changes colour and is a firm, spreadable consistency.

Royal icing

Shop-bought royal icing mixes give great results in a hurry, and taste just fine, but if you want to make your own royal icing at home just follow this simple recipe.

- ♥ 250g (9oz) icing (confectioners') sugar
- ♥ 1 large egg white
- ♥ ½ tsp lemon juice

1. Separate your egg white carefully, making sure not to include any broken eggshell.

2. Mix the egg white together with the lemon juice in a large bowl and begin to add the sugar gradually.

3. Beat the sugar and egg white together between each addition using an electric hand mixer.

4. Continue to beat the mixture for several minutes until the icing stands up in soft peaks. At this point the icing is ready to pipe.

5. If you want stiffer royal icing add more sugar; for runny royal icing (for flooding cookies) add water a few drops at a time and mix thoroughly until the desired consistency is achieved.

6. Cover your royal icing with cling film (plastic wrap), or place in an airtight container, and store it in the fridge until ready to use.

Sugarpaste (rolled fondant)

Sugarpaste is a sweet, thick, opaque paste that is soft, pliable, easily coloured and extremely versatile. Ready-made sugarpaste can be bought from supermarkets and cake-decorating suppliers, and is available in the whole colour spectrum. It is also easy and inexpensive to make your own.

- ♥ 60ml (4 tbsp) cold water
- ♥ 20ml (4 tsp) powdered gelatine
- ♥ 125ml (4fl oz) liquid glucose
- ♥ 15ml (1 tbsp) glycerine
- ♥ 1kg (2¼lb) icing (confectioners') sugar, sieved, plus extra for dusting

1   Place the water in a small bowl, sprinkle over the gelatine and soak until spongy.

2   Stand the bowl over a pan of hot, but not boiling, water and stir until the gelatine is dissolved. Add the glucose and glycerine, stirring until well blended and runny.

3   Put the icing (confectioners') sugar in a bowl. Make a well in the centre and slowly pour in the liquid ingredients, stirring constantly.

4   Turn out on to a surface dusted with icing (confectioners') sugar and knead until smooth, sprinkling with extra icing (confectioners') sugar if the paste becomes too sticky. The paste can be used immediately or wrapped and stored until required.

Tip: Store sugarpaste in thick plastic bags in an airtight container

Flower paste (petal/gum paste)

Available commercially from sugarcraft suppliers, flower paste can be bought in white and a range of colours. There are many varieties available so try a few to see which you prefer. Alternatively, it is possible to make your own, but it is a time-consuming process and you will need a heavy-duty mixer.

♥ 500g (1lb 2oz) icing (confectioners') sugar

♥ 15ml (1 tbsp) gum tragacanth

♥ 25ml (1½ tbsp) cold water

♥ 10ml (2 tsp) powdered gelatine

♥ 10ml (2 tsp) liquid glucose

♥ 15ml (1 tbsp) white vegetable fat (shortening)

♥ 1 medium egg white

1 Sieve the icing (confectioners') sugar and gum tragacanth into the greased mixing bowl of a heavy-duty mixer (the grease eases the strain on the mixer).

2 Place the water in a small bowl, sprinkle over the gelatine and soak until spongy.

3 Stand the bowl over a pan of hot (but not boiling) water and stir until the gelatine has dissolved. Add the glucose and white fat to the gelatine and continue heating until all the ingredients are melted and mixed.

4 Add the glucose mixture and egg white to the icing (confectioners') sugar. Beat the mixture slowly until mixed, then increase the speed until the paste becomes white and stringy.

5 Grease your hands and remove the paste from the bowl. Stretch it several times and then knead together. Place in a plastic bag and store in an airtight container. Leave to mature for at least 12 hours.

Tempering chocolate

Chocolate contains cocoa butter crystals and tempering is a process of heating chocolate so that these crystals are uniform. Correctly tempered chocolate will produce an end result that is smooth-tasting, crisp, even-coloured and shiny, while incorrectly tempered chocolate produces a dull or streaky end result often referred to as a 'bloom', which while not inedible, does look unsightly and will taste grainy. Incorrectly tempered chocolate will not set very well, will 'bend' rather than 'snap', and will not release easily from moulds, so before placing chocolate into a mould ensure it is correctly tempered.

How to temper chocolate

The simplest method is to purchase chocolate couverture callets or buttons, which have already been through one of the processes of tempering. With extreme care, these can be melted in a small plastic bowl in the microwave in short 10 second bursts on full power (850w), mixing thoroughly between each interval.

For chocolate buttercream, first add 2 tablespoons of cocoa powder (unsweetened cocoa) to 1–2 tablespoons of milk, then add just enough of this mixture to the buttercream to maintain its firm spreadable consistency.

Sugarpaste and modelling paste

Sugarpaste is available in many different colours. However, to get exact shades, you can use colouring paste to colour white sugarpaste. Place a little paste colour onto the end of a cocktail stick (toothpick) or a larger amount onto the end of a palette knife. Add to the paste and knead in thoroughly, adding more until you have the correct result. Be careful with pale colours, as only a little colour is needed.

Modelling paste is basically a stiffer version of sugarpaste that enables you to mould larger, less delicate shapes. It isn't as strong and won't dry out as quickly. You can buy ready-made modelling paste, but it is really simple and cheaper to make your own using CMC. This is a powder that is kneaded into the sugarpaste; use about 1 teaspoon per 300g (10½oz) icing.

Covering a round cake

To achieve a neat appearance for your finished cake it pays to take a little time to achieve a perfectly smooth finish.

1. To level off the cake place a cake board into the base of the tin in which the cake was baked so that when the cake is placed on top the outer edge of the cake is level with the tin and the dome will protrude above. Take a long sharp knife and cut the dome from the cake, keeping the knife against the tin. This will ensure the cake is completely level.

2. Cut the sponge into layers if you wish to add a filling. Using a small palette knife, spread a small amount of buttercream onto the cake board and stick down the bottom layer. Fill your cake layer(s) with buttercream and jam if you are using.

3. Cover the sides and top of the layered cake with a thin, even layer of buttercream. Refrigerate for at least an hour before covering with sugarpaste.

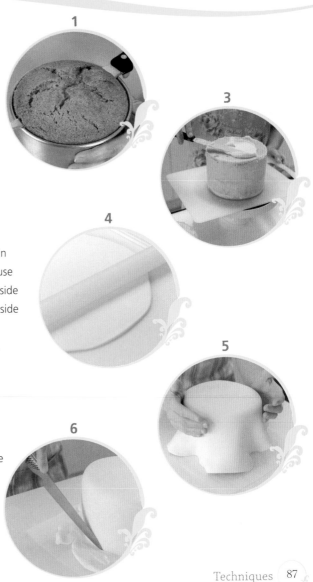

4. Knead the sugarpaste until it is soft. Roll it out with a large non-stick rolling pin on a large non-stick board, set over a non-stick mat. Use spacers to give you the correct depth – about 5mm ($^3/_{16}$in). Try to keep the shape round so that it will fit over your cake easily.

5. Pick the sugarpaste up on your rolling pin and lay it over your cake. Quickly but carefully use your hands to smooth it around and down the side of the cake. Pull the sugarpaste away from the side of the cake as you go until you reach the base. Try to push out any air bubbles that may occur.

6. When the icing is on, use a smoother in a circular motion to go over the top of the cake. For the side of the cake, go around in forward circular movements, almost cutting the excess paste at the base. Trim the excess with a small, sharp knife and smooth once more.

Icing cake boards

Covering the base cake board with sugarpaste makes a huge difference to the finished cake. By carefully choosing the right colour for the icing, the board can be incorporated into the design of the cake itself.

Moisten the board with some water. Roll out the sugarpaste to 4mm (a generous ⅛in). Pick the icing up on the rolling pin and lay it over the cake board. Place the board either on a turntable or bring it towards the edge of the work surface so that the icing is hanging down over it. Use your smoother in a downwards motion to cut a smooth edge around the board. Cut away any excess. Finish by smoothing the top using circular movements to achieve a flat and perfectly smooth surface for your cake to sit on. Leave to dry overnight.

Assembling tiered cakes

Stacking cakes on top of one another is not a difficult process, but it needs to be done in the right way so that you can rest assured that the cake is structurally sound. For a round cake a minimum of three hollow plastic dowels are required. These are very sturdy and easily cut to the correct height.

1. Mark the cake where the dowels should go. These need to be positioned well inside the diameter of the cake to be stacked on top. Push a dowel into the cake where it has been marked. Using an edible pen, mark the dowel where it meets the top of the cake.

2. Remove the dowel and cut it at the mark with a serrated knife. Cut the other dowels to the same height and insert them all into the cake.

1

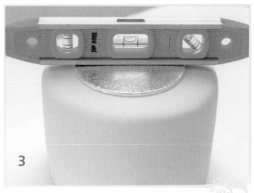

3

2

4. Stick your base cake onto the centre of your iced cake board with some stiff royal icing. Allow the icing to set for a few minutes before stacking on the next tier.

4

3. Place a cake board on top of the dowels and check that they are equal in height by using a spirit level.

Using buttercream

Using buttercream is the simplest way to decorate cupcakes. To get each cake looking perfect, you will need a little practice. You can pipe the topping using a large plastic piping (pastry) bag, making a peak or swirl with either a plain or star-shaped tube (tip). Alternatively, simply use a palette knife to spread the topping on evenly to create a nice domed top.

to create a swirl ...

1 Place the piping tube (tip) in a large piping (pastry) bag, then fill half the bag with your chosen topping. Twist the top of the bag to seal.

2 Holding the bag vertically, start at the centre of the cupcake. Apply pressure to the bag and then move the tube (tip) to the edge of the cupcake and around the centre of the cake in an anti-clockwise direction.

to create a peak ...

1 Hold the bag vertically above the centre of the cupcake. Keeping the bag still, apply pressure to the bag and allow the icing to spread towards the edge of the cupcake.

2 Once it has spread as far as you wish, start to slowly lift the bag while maintaining an even pressure. When finished, release the pressure and remove the bag.

Using royal icing

Royal icing is used to cover cupcakes and cookies, as well as for piping and stencilling designs. In order to pipe the icing easily, you may need to add a tiny amount of water so that the consistency is a bit softer. For stencilling, you will need a thicker consistency to ensure that the icing doesn't bleed underneath.

making a piping (pastry) bag ...

1 Cut two equal triangles from a large square piece of parchment paper. As a guide, for small bags cut from 15–20cm (6–8in) square paper and for large bags cut from 30–35cm (12–14in) square paper.

2 Keeping the centre point towards you with the longest side furthest away, curl the right-hand corner inwards and bring the point to meet the centre point. Adjust your hold so that you have the two points together between your right thumb and index finger.

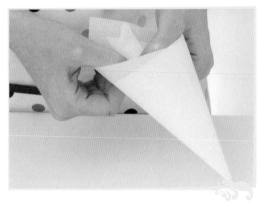

3 With your left hand, curl the left point inwards, bringing it across the front and around to the back of the other two points in the centre of the cone. Adjust your grip again so that you are now holding the three points together with both your thumbs and index fingers.

4 Tighten the cone-shaped bag by gently rubbing your thumb and index fingers forwards and backwards until you have a sharp tip at the end of the bag.

5 Carefully fold the back of the bag (where all the points meet) inwards, making sure you press hard along the fold. Repeat this to make sure it is really secure.

Piping with royal icing ...

1 Fill the piping (pastry) bag until it is no more than one-third full. Fold the top over, away from the join, until you have a tight and well-sealed bag. It's important to hold the bag in the correct way. Guide the bag with your index finger.

2 Touch the tube (tip) down, then lift the bag up in a smooth movement, squeezing gently. Decrease the pressure and touch it back down to the point where you want the icing to finish. Try not to drag the icing along. Use a template as a guide where possible.

3 To pipe dots, squeeze the icing out gently until you have the dot the size you require. Stop squeezing, then lift the bag. If there is a peak in the icing, use a damp brush to flatten it down.

Using cutters

There is a whole host of specialist sugarcraft cutters available in various shapes, sizes and designs. They are very simple to use and the results can be quite dramatic! There are two techniques for using cutters:

Cutting simple shapes ...

1 Press down onto your paste with the cutter, wiggle the cutter fractionally from side to side to give a cleaner cut.

2 Remove the excess paste, and ideally leave your paste on your work board for a minute or two before lifting it with a palette knife.

Cutting intricate shapes ...

1 To get a clean cut, rather than pressing a cutter into the paste, place the paste over the cutter and roll over with a rolling pin.

2 Run your finger over the edges of the cutter, then turn the cutter over and carefully press out the paste using a soft paintbrush.

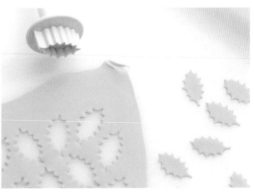

Suppliers

UK

The Pink Whisk Shop
Brunel House, Newton Abbot
Devon, TQ12 4PU
Tel: 0844 880 5852
www.thepinkwhiskshop.com

Blue Ribbons
29 Walton Road, East Molesey, Surrey,
KT8 0DH
Tel: 020 8941 1591
www.blueribbons.co.uk

The Cake Parlour
146 Arthur Road, London,
SW19 8AQ
Tel: 020 8947 4424
www.thecakeparlour.com

FMM Sugarcraft
Unit 7, Chancerygate Business Park,
Whiteleaf Road, Hemel Hempstead,
Herts, HP3 9HD
Tel: 01442 292970
www.fmmsugarcraft.com

Home Chocolate Factory
Unit 1750, SafeStore,
1,000 North Circular Road,
London, NW2 7JP
Tel: 020 8450 1523
www.homechocolatefactory.com

Knightbridge PME Ltd
Chadwell Heath Lane,
Romford, Essex, RN6 4NP
Tel: 020 8590 5959
www.cakedecoration.co.uk

Lindy's Cakes Ltd
Unit 2, Station Approach, Wendover,
Aylesbury, Buckinghamshire, HP22
6BN
Tel: 01296 622418
www.lindyscakes.co.uk

Maisie's World
840 High Lane, Chell, Stoke on Trent,
Staffordshire, ST6 6HG
Tel: 01782 876090
www.maisieparrish.com

Orchard Products
51 Hallyburton Road, Hove,
East Sussex, BN3 7GP
Tel: 01273 419418
www.orchardproducts.co.uk

A Piece of Cake
18–20 Upper High Street, Thame,
Oxon , OX9 3EX
Tel: 01844 213428
www.sugaricing.com

Squire's Kitchen
3 Waverley Lane,
Farnham, Surrey,
GU9 8BB
Tel: 0845 6171 810
www.squires-shop.com

Sugarshack
Unit 12, Bowmans Trading Estate,
Westmoreland Road,
London, NW9 9RL
Tel: 020 8204 2994
www.sugarshack.co.uk

Tracey's Cakes Ltd
5 Wheelwright Road, Longwick,
Buckinghamshire, HP27 9ST
Tel: 01844 347147
www.traceyscakes.co.uk

US
All In One Bake Shop
8566 Research Boulevard,
Austin, TX 78758
Tel: 512 371 3401
www.allinonebakeshop.com

Chocolate Man
16580 35th Ave NE,
Lake Forest Park,
WA 98155-6606
Tel: 206 365 2025
www.chocolateman.com

Copper Gifts
900 North 32nd Street,
Parsons, KS 67357
Tel: 620 421 0654
www.coppergifts.com

Country Kitchen Sweet Art
4621 Speedway Drive Fort, Wayne,

IN 46825
Tel: 800 497 3927
www.countrykitchensa.com

First Impressions Molds
300 Business Park Way,
Suite A-200, Royal Palm
Beach, FL 33411
Tel: 561 784 7186
www.firstimpressionsmolds.com

Global Sugar Art
625 Route 3, Unit 3,
Plattsburgh,NY 12901
Tel: 518 561 3039
www.globalsugarart.com

New York Cake Supplies
56 West 22nd Street,
New York, NY 10010
Tel: 800 942 2539
www.nycake.com

Wilton Industries Inc.
2240 West 75th Street, Woodridge,
IL 60517
Tel: 800 794 5866
www.wilton.com

US cup measurements
If you prefer to use cup
measurements, please use the
following conversions. (Note: 1
Australian tbsp = 20ml)

liquid
1 tsp = 5ml
1 tbsp = 15ml
½ cup = 125ml/4fl oz
1 cup = 225ml/8fl oz

butter
1 tbsp = 15g/½oz
2 tbsp = 25g/1oz
½ cup/1 stick = 115g/4oz
1 cup/2 sticks = 225g/8oz

**caster (superfine) sugar/brown
sugar**
½ cup = 100g/3½oz
1 cup = 200g/7oz
icing (confectioners') sugar
1 cup = 115g/4oz

flour
1 cup = 140g/5oz
double (heavy) cream
1 cup = 225g/8oz

A DAVID & CHARLES BOOK
© F&W Media International, LTD 2013

David & Charles is an imprint of F&W Media
International, Ltd
Brunel House, Forde Close, Newton Abbot,
TQ12 4PU, UK

F&W Media International, Ltd is a subsidiary of
F+W Media, Inc
10151 Carver Road, Cincinnati OH45242, USA

First published in the UK and US in 2013
Published in the US as *Stitch Craft Create Quick Bakes*

Content, layout and photography © F&W Media
International, LTD 2013

The designers and publisher have made every effort to
ensure that all the instructions in the book are accurate
and safe, and therefore cannot accept liability for any
resulting injury, damage or loss to persons or property,
however it may arise.

Names of manufacturers and product ranges are
provided for the information of readers, with no
intention to infringe copyright or trademarks.

A catalogue record for this book is available from the
British Library.

ISBN-13: 978-1-4463-0390-0 paperback (UK)
ISBN-10: 1-4463-0390-X paperback (UK)

ISBN-13: 978-1-4463-0396-2 paperback (US)
ISBN-10: 1-4463-0396-9 paperback (US)

Printed in China by RR Donnelley
for F&W Media International, LTD
Brunel House, Forde Close, Newton Abbot,
TQ12 4PU, UK

10 9 8 7 6 5 4 3 2 1

Publisher: Alison Myer
Multi-Channel Content Editor: James Brooks
Art Editor: Charly Bailey
Project Photographer: Sian Irvine
Production Manager: Bev Richardson

F+W Media, Inc. publishes high-quality books on a wide
range of subjects. For more great book ideas visit:
www.stitchcraftcreate.co.uk